RANCH DOG

A Tribute to the Working Dog in the American West

RANCH DOG

BY
MARIANNE MURDOCK

PHOTOGRAPHY BY NANCY BURGESS

Willow Creek
P R E S S

MINOCQUA, WISCONSIN

Published by Willow Creek Press
P.O. Box 147, Minocqua, Wisconsin 54548

For information on other Willow Creek Press titles, call 1-800-850-9453

Library of Congress Cataloging-in-Publication Data
Ranch Dog : a tribute to the working dog in the American West / [compiled] by Marianne Murdock ; photography by Nancy Burgess.
p. cm.
ISBN 1-57223-289-7
1. Herding dogs—West (U.S.) 2. Livestock protection dogs—West (U.S.)
I. Murdock, Marianne.   II. Burgess, Nancy.
SF428.6.R36 2000
636.73—dc21
00-009011

Printed in Canada

This book is dedicated to my mother,
Jane Murdock Jeremko

In Loving Memory

Contents

Acknowledgments

The inspiration for this book came from a photograph of my two departed dogs, Bill and Pokie. The photo was taken while on a road trip through the West. My ex-sweetheart and I had tethered the dogs to a split-rail fence to give a herd of deer, trying to get a drink from a nearby lake, some peace and quiet. When the film was developed and I saw that shot, my words were "they look like ranch dogs!" The seed was planted.

Though I've yet to meet a dog who can read, I want to express my heartfelt thanks to all the dogs who unknowingly participated in this project. Without the dogs, there is no book. Thanks, too, to the stock animals who allowed us to intrude into their daily lives.

My thanks to the ranch owners, ranchers and wranglers. It was a pleasure to meet you all, and your willingness to allow us to hang out while you worked is greatly appreciated.

A very special thanks to all the poets who graciously provided material. The poetry is the heartbeat of this book.

For the hospitality and great food provided by Dave and Donna Zieler and Steven Bray at their lovely ranch in Wyoming, a very special thanks. It was so good to catch up.

To my best friend, Janet David, who put up with my "ranch dogging" on our "chicks on the road" trip to Taos, thank you! (That feral pack is right behind you, headin' down the wash!) And to the Outback—great pizza!

To the folks at Sharlot Hall Museum, the Prescott Cowboy Poets Gathering and Bradshaw Mountain Photo: thanks for all the help. A special thanks to Randy Swedlund.

To George Huey and Christina Watkins: what can I say? Your expertise and willingness to answer ALL of my questions is really appreciated! Your encouragement meant so much! Thanks for all of your help.

To Whitney and Tom Nickerson: thanks for taking care of Cruiser while I was on the road!

Thanks to Jay Dusard for taking a look at the photos and offering his advice.

To Frank S. Coburn, D.V.M. for giving me access to the computer after hours and for not firing me when I needed *another* week off.

To "Alaska John" Eldridge for supporting the arts. O.K., here it is: I couldn't have done it without you! I also want to mention "Scooter."

To Montgomery Higgins, also a patron of the arts, thank you!

To my good friend Martha Marine: "How do!"

A special thanks to my family: To my favorite sister, Jan Graham — I love you so much! To my biggest fans — my "Dahling" Aunt Mary and Uncle Hal Christensen who have always believed in me. To my incredible Aunt Anne Harasik who opened an amazing door to me twenty years ago. To my "Darlin'" Maxx Murdock Johnson for his photographic assistance in Elko and for leading us safely through a desert wind storm one evening — I love you! To Rex Johnson for moving right out of his abode for several nights in order to give us a place to crash. (And food!) To Bill and Karrie Christensen for dinner and fine company. To Hal and Sharon Christensen for offering the same. To the "brood" belonging to Bill and Karrie and Hal and Sharon, for sitting through the poetry reading at the old homestead in "Badger," Utah. To my dazzlingly brilliant and very good-looking cousin Dana Murdock for her encouragement and very fine culinary skills. To my dear, departed grandmother and grandfather, Abe and Vie Murdock, whose love of the West osmotically had me refusing to remove my holster and guns while down with the chicken "pops" at the tender age of four.

And to my dearest, departed mother, Jane Murdock Jaremko, for allowing me to exercise my creativity at all times. I miss you more than words can tell.

A very special thanks to Nancy Burgess for her willingness to step into this without knowing where it was going. Thank you for your wonderful photographs, your vision, your support, your incredible organizational skills, your patience, editing, and the ability to get a bur under my saddle when needed! Also, congratulations!

To Jim Burgess for hauling us to the airport and back, and for explaining that the departing planes were partaking in a "controlled ascent!" Also, for your editorial and computer expertise and for the time you spent getting it all on one of those little disks!

And finally, to Willow Creek Press who made this dream a reality and who allowed me to include this incredibly lengthy acknowledgment!

To anyone I may have overlooked, my sincere apology. It was a long journey!

—M.M.

Introduction

IN EIGHTEENTH CENTURY SPAIN, A SPELUNKER WAS INVESTIGATING AN UNDERGROUND cave at a depth of 300 feet. During the cave explorer's descent he heard a pitiful cry coming from the darkness. After overcoming his initial apprehension, he decided to seek out the source of the cry. It happened to be coming from an old sheep herding dog who lay 200 feet down the incline. Determined to save the old dog, the spelunker solicited the help of his two companions who were waiting at the entrance to the cave. After six hours of hard work, the men successfully freed the dog from its deep, dark, consequential habitat.

Evidently, the dog had been purposefully tossed into the cave by its master, who was enraged by the cur's habit of nipping at the sheep. As the story goes, disposed of and presumably left for dead, the dog had miraculously landed in a small underground lake, surviving the fall and finding itself surrounded by partially intact carcasses of discarded stock animals. These carcasses would be periodically thrown into the pit. This unlikely environment sustained the life of this poor dog for three years!

The truly profound link in this story concerning the dog's loyalty, is that once the dog was freed from its proposed burial pit, it went directly back to its original herding ground and began to work. The dog stood ready to serve the very master who had, three years earlier, thrown the canine to what he had presumed would be the animal's death![†]

The loyalty of a dog to its master and livelihood has been depicted throughout history for centuries. The amount of attention that the *L. canis* has received through the visual and written works of man proves without a doubt that this is truly a unique species.

[†]From *Life, History and Magic of the Dog*, Robert Laffont, Madison Square Press.

Historians and paleontologists have found evidence that the use of herding dogs may be traced back to approximately 500 BC when, in Europe, it is thought that the Dingo dog was used to flush out game, bringing it into closer proximity for the hunter. It is believed that seafaring men brought the Dingo to Australia. Never having been truly domesticated, the Dingo today is one of the true wild dogs of the world and is now actually an unwelcome guest to a sheepherder's flock.

No one knows for sure exactly when men and dogs became the peaceful companions they are today, but the depictions of several ancient Egyptian hieroglyphics may indicate that the two species, even then, shared kindred spirits.

In ancient Mexico, the dog had the unfortunate and involuntary role of accompanying its master into the world of the afterlife. The dog would be put to death and be placed beside the body of its master so that the dead man could reach the afterworld safely.

A lot has changed since then. In order to get an accurate idea of the world of the working dog on a Western ranch today, specifically the herders, one must see these animals in action. The portraits of these working dogs hopefully capture the integrity, personality, loyalty and love of work that these dogs possess.

The working ranch dog represents many different breeds of dog. On occasion,

13

one will run into a "breed" which seems to have been cultivated through totally unsupervised canine courtship! It appears though, in the American West, the most popular breeds for cattle, sheep and goat herding are the Catahoula Hound, the Queensland cattle dog (heeler), the Border collie, the Australian shepherd, the black mouth cur and of course, the occasional mongrel.

Some of these dogs were incredibly friendly and welcoming, but for the most part, they take the guarding of their stock, territory, cowboys, and cowgirls very seriously. They were often stranger-shy and would take on a guarded posture until they received the knowing command from their master to begin their work. The time to really get to know these dogs is when they are on the job. When in their element, doing what they have been bred and trained to do, there are few things that can compare to the sheer joy and amazement one experiences while looking on in disbelief. There are, of course, some cowboys and girls that will tell you that the only good cowdog is a dead one, but a good number of ranchers swear by their dogs, as well as *at* them on occasion!

Also included is some very special cowboy poetry. The images offered in these uniquely crafted poems are varied. Some will beckon tears, some will beckon laughter. Hopefully, some of these poems will remind the reader of a dog they have known or loved.

The freedom, the landscapes, the horses, livestock and riders, all help to create the adventurous and beautiful lifestyle that belongs to these dogs. It's sometimes hard and very brutal, certainly not without its dangers, but on a good day, in good open country, things can run quite smoothly; provided, of course, that you've got a few good Ranch Dogs around!

The Bath

by Marianne Murdock

Now it don't happen often
Maybe once't a year
Sometimes that "cur" just needs a bath
So's you can see 'im clear
'Cause after a month out on the range
They all get to lookin' brown
Ya can't tell "Spec" from "Digger"
Makes it hard to call 'em down

Now all ya need's a bucket
Some water and some soap
And the most important thing of all
A good, short, sturdy rope
It only takes ten minutes
Give or take a few
An' ya gotta be fast on yer feet
Or he'll shake all wet on you

An' that mutt'll be obligin'
As he looks you in the eye
He'll take 'is shiny canine coat
An' head straight fer the nearest "pie"

A BAR V RANCH

Skull Valley, Arizona

WHEN YOU FIRST GET TO THE A BAR V RANCH IN SKULL VALLEY, ARIZONA, something comes over you. All of a sudden you want to slow down and take everything in. The unique landscape of this desert valley, the smell of wild sage on the hillsides, and the words that fall out of Bob Pulley's mouth like friendly molasses, all create a sense of peace that only those who live off the land can know.

Bob has been the foreman on this ranch for more than twenty-five years. His wife Sonia often joins her husband in the running of this ranch. They run about a hundred head of cattle down on this spread, mostly Brahma and Hereford, mixed.

Bob has also been raising Catahoula hounds for twenty-two years. Though the Catahoula is thought to be a descendant of the mastiff-type dogs brought to America by Spanish explorers, the true origin of this unusual dog has been lost.

The "Cat," which this dog is sometimes referred to, can be traced to a region in Louisiana called Blue Lakes, or Parish of Catahoula (meaning beautiful clear water). Known for being aggressive and tough, these dogs were popular for herding wild pigs in the swampy lands of Louisiana. This breed is also known as the Catahoula leopard dog, hog dog, or cur, depending on the region from which it comes. While these dogs are sturdy and strong-willed, they also posses a sensitivity and fierce loyalty to their owners.

The coat of a Catahoula can vary greatly. Primarily merle with black or tan mottling, some Cats have mostly black coats while some have two-toned color such as Bob's "catch dog," Ring. Ring gets his name from the shock of white that circles his neck.

The dogs on the A Bar V are probably among the friendliest, as well as the most entertaining. Bob had a fairly easy job ahead of him, just rounding up a few stray cows not far from home. The atmosphere was easy-going until he freed up his two dogs, Bubba and Ring. These dogs are both quite young and so incredibly robust

that it tires one to simply stand there and watch as they warm up for work. While Bob saddles up his horse, Bubba and Ring circle the perimeter of the entire corral about a hundred times. Of course getting over-heated in the Arizona desert is not a big deal, providing you've got a horse trough full of water to jump into! Once the fore-man has mounted his horse, it's all about "gettin' the job done." Through whistles and commands, Bob lets the two eager canines know exactly what he expects them to do. They follow the boss and watch closely for his next command.

Ring has a tendency to get a little too aggressive, which is why he's referred to as a catch dog. Bob says it refers to the undesirable habit that some of these dogs have of trying to literally lead the cattle by the nose. Ring is sometimes fitted with a special wire muzzle while herding, as he still hasn't learned all of the disciplines of being a Ranch Dog. The muzzle is roomy enough for panting and drinking water, but not for catching a cow's nostrils between a dog's teeth. As the trainer says, "There are a few ranchers out there that'll tell you these Catahoulas aren't good for herdin'. They don't have much *whoa* in 'em!" However, Bob's best herding dogs have all been Cats, which is probably one of the reasons he chooses to raise them.

After a while, the rider returns and corrals the strays. At a slow walk behind him are two dogs, finally out of steam and ready to settle down into the coolness of the evening, along with the setting Arizona sun.

SURE THING

By Stan Young

Love the poetry sure
The whack and ring
Slosh an' drizzle
Snarl smash an' tear

The bumping and twining
In the gurgle of time
Treading wine and brine
Both mating and hating

So I chide myself to seek reality
And remember the sound and look of words
As they touch and clump are but few
Of the clues I'll be needing

Reward and incitement for my dogs sure
Scent for tracking a wily old bull
All around these mountains
Important sure better check it out
Like manure steaming on the trail

S BAR S RANCH
Kamas, Utah

S-S

As Interstate 80 stretches to the east of Salt Lake City, the golden foothills of the Uinta mountain range roll past the town of Park City and the frenetic pace of urban life is quickly left behind. In the west, one only has to drive a short distance from any major city to find the open, lush valleys and eminent mountain ranges that exist around the perimeters of small ranching towns such as Kamas, Utah.

The S Bar S Ranch sprawls out along Kamas Valley, among the slopes of the Uinta Mountains, creating a sublime home for 350-500 head of horses. The owner of the S Bar S, Tom Simpson, breeds and trains quarter horses and Overo Paints. While the ranch also runs about 500 head of cattle, the horses are the first love at the S Bar S. Tom Simpson's family has been on this ranch since the early 1940s. It has a rich history and a relaxed atmosphere. There is no doubt that the people living and working on this land are comfortable and confident in its operation.

The operation goes smoothly with the help of Tom's family, a few hands and, of course, several ranch dogs. When it comes to good herding dogs, Tom Simpson's breed of choice is the Australian shepherd. The rancher claims that an Aussie can learn more in one second than a Blue Heeler can learn in a lifetime. He also says that if he were as smart as an Aussie, he could "teach 'em to talk."

Tom's favorite working dog is a male Australian shepherd he simply calls Aussie. The dogs' registered name is Tom of Rigby, but work on the S Bar S favors a more lax disposition. Aussie was born on the ranch about nine years ago and is still going strong.

One of Aussie's impressive achievements, along with several of the other ranch dogs, is his ability to flush out a single horse, commanded by name, from a group of about sixty head. The dogs are evidently able to do this after only one working session with a particular horse. This talent is especially helpful during the breeding season when the ranch breeds several hundred mares during about four months in the spring and summer. When they need a particular mare out of a large group, they'll send one of the dogs in to take her out.

There have been quite a few Australian shepherds and Aussie mixes bred on the ranch over the years. Aussie has sired his share with his mate Smilin' Britches, another Aussie who acquired her name through the habit of "affectionately" baring her teeth any time she gets fussed over by humans. Smilin' Britches has produced most of the dogs from the S Bar S.

Tom's son, Scott, who ranches here full-time, works with a two-year-old Aussie by the name of Poopah. Tom feels that this young male dog may be one of the best they've produced. If Poopah turns out to be as good as the Simpsons think he will, then they plan to breed him with a blue merle Aussie they've recently purchased by the name of Maggie. Smilin' Britches has done her share. She now gets to go into retirement and watch her offspring from the comforts of the shaded lawn around the property.

Tom's daughter, Chris, also works the ranch when she's not called in to work as a flight attendant for a national airline. Chris has been working with her new dog, Boots, who is a young black and white Aussie. Though a bit overzealous, Boots, with just a little less confidence than her older and more experienced cohorts, stays by Chris like a shadow until she's given the command to keep the horses in check. At that time, she will loop around to the band and herd them according to her orders. She is an eager student and will no doubt grow into a fine working dog.

Marie is a high school student who works on the S Bar S whenever she gets the chance. Though young, she is a confident wrangler and works in synchronized movements along with her Queensland heeler, Smilin' Boots. Boots is no stranger to work and performs her routines with an innate ability. She is smaller in stature than the Aussies that dominate the spread, but there is no doubt about her capabilities. Though the horses tower above the little dog, she goes about her work fearlessly.

The S Bar S also uses three-wheelers on their land, usually for quick routine checks on the livestock after they've been herded to their respective pastures or corrals. The dogs seem to enjoy jumping into their masters' laps for a free ride to the check point. Tom says the motorized vehicles also help to desensitize the pups to unexpected noises on the ranch. From November 1 to about May 1, it takes two people and their dogs, working sixteen-hour days, to keep the S Bar S running smoothly. Most of the 500 head of cattle are moved to a warmer climate during the winter, but the horses remain and must be tended to during the harsh Utah winters. A few of the cattle are kept on the ranch during this time to help with the training of the horses. The dogs are an integral part of that training. Tom says that when the dogs are working the horses, he will command them to "talk" or to be "quiet" as they work. The barking will get the attention of the horse and the dog can then coax the animal to get the designated chore accomplished. When the cattle are being worked, the opposite is true. Tom prefers to work the dogs in silence as the barking tends to spook the herd.

The ranch also serves as a boarding facility for horses owned by people in the "big city." The ranch hands and their dogs go about their daily routines undaunted by the comings and goings of horse owners and visitors. It's a friendly place, a peaceful and beautiful spot. As the sun sets on the horizon after snaking across the valley, the ranch dogs recline in various places under the huge oaks that surround the old Victorian house the Simpsons call home.

DOG

by John Milstead

I don't think I remember the exact direction
He walked in from the fog
But for more than 17 years
I called that mutt my dog

He got here just a mess of fur
All tongue and feet and hair
But Alpo and me and table scraps
Made him big as a bear

He hated cows, see, one had kicked him
When he was just a pup
But he musta loved me 'cause ever mornin'
He'd go out and round 'em up

He'd bark and growl and snap and fuss
And them cows would belch and cough
And they'd go trottin' in the corral
They were scared they'd tick him off

He loved to ride in that pickup of mine
Fur Flyin', mouth open wide
It could rain or snow or sleet or hail
I still couldn't get him inside

I'd wash that pickup every week
To get off the mud and the mire
And he'd go 'round when I'd finished
And pee on every tire

Those 17 years just went too fast
And his eyesight got less keen
It was hard to think I was 37
And he was 119

One day it got so he just wouldn't eat
And he left all the water in his pail
But through all his pain, when I came near
He could always wag his tail

I could see that he'd herded his last cow
And followed his last rabbit track
So I carried him out to the pickup
For his last ride in the back

I buried him up the hill from the house
It's the direction I most like to walk
So it's handy to stop off there for a while
Just to set and have us a talk

Even though it was somethin' that I had to do
I don't mind tellin' ya, son
Takin' that old dog on his last ride
Was the hardest thing I've ever done

A funny thing happened the other day
And I don't understand it just yet
But the last time I came back down from the hill
All four tires on my pickup were wet

The vet was kind, and the end was quick
And he probably felt no pain
But I cried every one of those 26 miles
When I carried him back home again

(In memory of Chief, the best dog ever)

WARREN LIVE STOCK COMPANY
Cheyenne, Wyoming

7XL

THE WARREN LIVE STOCK COMPANY IS ONE OF THE LARGER SHEEP AND CATTLE ranches in the United States. The company has extensive land holdings both in Colorado and Wyoming. Founded in 1874 by Francis E. Warren (who was Wyoming's first governor and who served in the United States Senate for nearly 40 years), the company was purchased by the Etchepare family in 1973. Paul

Etchepare served as managing partner and chairman of the board of this impressive family business from 1963 until his passing in the Spring of 1997 at the age of 86. His sons, Paul and John, along with other family members, are integral parts of this large operation. The Warren Live Stock Company currently farms wheat, and raises beef, lamb and wool.

The Etchepare family is descended from the Basque region of the French Pyrenees Mountains. Famous for their sheep herding, many Basques immigrated to the U.S., following their dreams to the "land of opportunity." In 1890, one of those immigrants, seventeen-year-old John Etchepare, Sr. found his way west and worked as a sheepherder in California and then as a lumberjack in Montana. As the story goes, young John, while logging in the mountains, heard what he considered to be beautiful music, the distant tinkling of sheep bells. He slammed his ax into a stump and followed the sound to the source. There, in the middle of the majestic mountain forest, John Etchepare found a flock of sheep and another Basque who was

working for a Montana rancher. John soon began to work for the same outfit, eventually striking out on his own with a band of sheep. He became a successful rancher in his own right. Later, he returned to his native France and married his childhood sweetheart. He returned to the western United States with her. It was during a family visit to Ustaritz in the French Pyrenees when Mrs. Etchepare gave birth to their son, Paul, on January 25, 1911. From this humble beginning in a small French village, Paul would become, fifty years later, the president and owner of the Warren Live Stock Company.

The company has become well known for its "twinning" Warhill sheep (named after the two men who developed the breed). Over the years, through careful research and scientific study, the ranch has produced a magnificent line of sheep whose bloodline boasts the common occurrence of multiple births. This results in an economical and environmentally supportive lambing operation. The company also prides itself with the most conscientious shepherding of these animals.

Amidst the vast open rangelands outside of Cheyenne, Wyoming, are scattered the company's lone bands of sheep and their caretakers. Depending on the time of year, there are anywhere from ten to seventeen bands of sheep on the Warren Live Stock property, each comprised of fifteen hundred to two thousand head of stock. There is one shepherd per band of sheep and each uses a working dog.

Victor Alderete is one such shepherd. His homeland is Peru and his grandfather was a Basque. Victor and his dog, a one-year-old Border collie named Savino, will work here in the United States for three years before returning to his family in Peru. He will make a good wage and be able to return home with substantial earnings. Almost all of the shepherds come from Peru or Mexico to work for the ranch. They work under a federal contract which allows an eleven month stay that may be extended up to a maximum of three years.

It seems a lonely job with this flock of sheep out in the middle of nowhere, with only Savino for company and a small shepherd's wagon for shelter. Victor, although he speaks little English, communicates that he is content and he seems to be a happy and easygoing man.

One of Savino's jobs, other than herding and keeping the flock together as they graze the ranges, is to keep the band safe from predators at night. Savino is a shy dog and has no interest in meeting strangers. He wears his post as naturally as one would take to a warm blanket made from the wool of this very flock. He is eager to follow Victor and eager to respond to the shepherd's commands. If a sheep breaks from the band, Savino will look to Victor with anticipation, waiting to be instructed to retrieve the animal. Man and dog work closely together, with Victor sometimes using whistles to communicate his instructions. The only moment that this dog is not keenly attuned to his work is when an old, well-traveled truck rumbles over a broad, low hill, seemingly out of the clear blue sky. The driver, another shepherd named Antonia Saturnino, is on his way back to his camp and stops to exchange greetings, providing a brief but pleasant social break in the quiet world of the shepherds. Antonia's ranch dog, Soruyo, is an interesting cross of a Border collie and a basset hound. Soruyo, whose basset genes are obviously predominant, excitedly elevates his stature on the edge of the truck bed to greet Savino, his friend and colleague (perhaps that should be spelled "collie-gue"). The two dogs exchange their greeting as only dogs can, and then Antonia and Soruyo continue on to their camp.

Victor and Savino work smoothly to bring their band down to the watering trough for a drink before heading to the top of a knoll for a break at the shepherder's wagon. The sheep continue to graze the low rolling hillsides as Savino keeps an ever-watchful eye on his stock. Thus, one of the many traditions of the Warren Live Stock Company lives on.

DOG'S LIFE

By Stan Young

I've watched these pups come along
seemingly separate balls of energy
Just rolling chances
So unassuming they can't remember
needin' their feet for dancin'
But mostly dreamin'
Some out-of-body experience
as individual sense unfolds
and so does activity grow until
It's play with me . . . look at me
then let me specifically out to pee.

Young Heeler stockdogs crave workin'
feel the creative impulse so strong
they must respond and shape reality
by persuadin' other critters to mind.
All they don't know is when to quit.
Maybe it's blood from the dingo side
the way they just latch on the idea
Lovin' the job and workin' so hard
they'll seem to forget themselves
and become like disembodied forces
Usually divin' in there for heels
but cows or sows or horses bossin' 'em
aren't keepin' their noses pristine either.

Never forget seein' the one I called Nikki
front a four hundred pound sow on the charge
grab an ear and throw 'er upside down
and she'd think smarter, and share it more
than other dogs I've been around.
Not long lived, workin' hard or otherwise
ten or eleven, and one mornin' they're gone.
My Nikki's eyes were night blind at eight

But she didn't tell me until one night
when I could see she'd hesitated
in trees away from the fire
at the Goodwin bedground on the Buzzard M.
Pushin' the beggar cows back from the horses
I hollered some dog lingo
And the way she cried out
It makes me ache today
always will, wantin'
so awful bad to help git 'em.

Tho later on she got day blind as well
she did okay around the home place
By nine they're slowin' down anyway
not takin' things quite so personal.
They're sleepin' more . . . yet a different sleep
Much deeper than the pups.
I'm bettin' the mix won't be unlike
the collective intelligence
Of the universe . . . mostly a long, far
Crooked runaway from consciousness.
Myself lately, I've come around to where
I can picture death as absentmindedness.

EL MONTE LODGE

Taos, New Mexico

Nestled in the valley below "Taos Mountain" sits a quaint little lodge surrounded by some of New Mexico's most magnificent old ranch country. Several years ago, the author happened on this lovely dwelling and upon seeing a wonderful dog, recumbent on the cool, tiled office floor, decided that the El Monte Lodge was the place to stay. Lady, whose lineage might have dictated that she be herding cattle, was about eight years old at the time. An Australian shepherd mix, with one blue eye, one brown, and sporting a beautifully mottled coat, had appointed herself concierge of the lodge. The owners at the time, George and Pat Schumacher, reported that Lady had become accustomed to following George around during his daily caretaking rounds of the little adobe dwellings which serve as the guest quarters. As George would go about his ground's keeping business and ensuring the guests had everything they needed, Lady would lazily follow in his path, knowing that his pockets were usually filled with dog biscuits. (Cowboys, take note.)

During the course of the day, Lady could be found in the office seeking refuge from the elements, or simply taking a break

from all of the attention that came her way via the visitors at the Lodge. As a new guest arrived, she would look up from her station to offer her approval. If one happend to have a treat in hand, that approval might be more immediate.

While Lady is not a typical herding dog like the others in this book, she was nonetheless a working dog, carrying out her duties as "keeper of the gate." She could also be seen chasing out the occasional wild animal (usually a rabbit) which found its way down from the beautiful surrounding wilderness.

These days, Lady spends her time in Rio Rancho playing with the Schumacher's granddaughters, Naomi and Caley. Pat Schumacher, now a widow, lives in Colorado with fond memories of the El Monte Lodge and the years spent in Taos, New Mexico.

The new owner of the Lodge reports that he has two dogs now on the premises and one canine visitor from town. It seems Lady has started a tradition at the El Monte.

WHITE-COLLARED WORKER

By Marianne Murdock

I've seen those curs, out blazin' the herds
Gettin' all roughed up
They take the trail of full resistance
Countin' on nature and luck

And while I'd have to say to the lot
As a dog lookin' on from afar
I admire their spunk and the cowboy's "bunk"
Though I'd just as soon blaze on laid tar

While my breedin' might govern the life I should lead
I've got to admit I've had choices
I'd much rather listen to my Master's "Chopin"
Than be subjected to the cowpuncher's voices

So yes, we're all workers
We've all got a job
Though some's a bit harder than others
And though I herd "lore" from a central cooled floor
I hail praise to my sisters and brothers

And alas, we as dogs
Who in some way are collared
I believe the forespokens' are blue
But I've worn this white one for many a year
Administratin's what I choose to do!

MATLI RANCH

Prescott, Arizona

I<small>T'S LIKE PASSING INTO A DIFFERENT ERA WHEN YOU APPROACH THE DIRT ROAD</small> turn-off to the Matli Ranch. To the northeast is a stand of giant cottonwoods that leans permanently in the direction of the wind. After about a mile of shallow dips and curves, you come to a homestead that's been there since before 1903. That was the year that Judy Matli's grandparents began ranching on this particular piece of Heaven on Earth.

Surrounding the modest house are unbelievably well-preserved wood structures still used by the woman who's been running this ranch for the past fifteen years, with the help of her dogs. Judy is down to three dogs now. She owns a grey and black speckled Catahoula/Aussie mix named "Spec," a tan and white Aussie mix named "Sally," and "Pepper," a black and white, six-month-old Border collie mix "in training."

On the first visit to the Matli Ranch, things were pretty quiet. The ranch woman was out herding cattle and there was no way of communicating to her that she may have company, as the ranch has no telephone. Suddenly surrounded by buildings unchanged for decades, it was as if we had stepped back in time. The well-tended flower and vegetable garden echoed a life lived simply. There was a comfortable looking screened porch in the shade of several fruit trees, a few large pens

housing various ranch dogs, a horse corral, and a chicken coop peppered with chickens, roosters and several recumbent cats, seemingly unaware that they were mingling with what should have been their natural prey.

The penned dogs greeted us through the chicken wire with excitement and guarded hesitation. One of the dogs on the ranch was not penned, but tethered just outside of one of the outbuildings. She was a very old Queensland heeler and she lay stoically, indifferent to the presence of strangers. She was a fixture there and it was evident that it would take a whole lot more than a couple of greenhorns to get her hackles up. "Shadow" was photographed on that first visit.

On the second trip to the ranch, Judy, with three broken ribs acquired while trying to repair a portion of the hay barn, was astride her horse, "Snoop," looking for a stray bull. When asked about the old Queensland, Judy nodded towards the west side of the old shed to a small, freshly dug grave. She told us that Shadow was sixteen years old when she died; Judy had adopted her from the animal shelter fourteen years earlier. The heeler had evidently been mistreated by her previous owners and Judy said that it took a while to earn the dog's trust. As it turned out, Shadow was the "best herdin' and loadin' dog" on the ranch for almost fourteen years.

After swapping dog stories near the ranch house for a while, the subject changed and Judy told us that the ranch had been sold to developers who had plans

for a subdivision. Judy's share of the ranch was not enough to keep "progress" at bay. It would take a lot more land to continue to move a hundred head of Beefmasters. She would be moving out in a few months. She left us with her brother's address in Texas — said he'd be able to get correspondence to her.

When it was time to leave, this cowgirl, with broken ribs and all, headed off on old Snoop, with Spec and Sally trailing faithfully along. There was still the matter of that stray bull to tend to.

SUBDIVIDED [For Judy Matli]

by Marianne Murdock

I was there just twice before
In nineteen ninety four and five
Although I'd never felt so still
I was never more alive
There's just somethin' 'bout a ranch
Born years and years ago
That makes you breathe a little deeper
Move a bit more slow
It's more than what the eye can see
The soul can see it too
The family that's lived on this land
Feels like kin to you

Now it's not yours, you're just a guest
But there's somethin' 'bout the air
That makes a body feel a part
Of all that's happened there
And there was nothin' fancy (yet)
Old wood and open land
And the humble voice of a cowgirl
With a rein in a weathered hand
And as she turned her gelding
Just slightly to one side
She said they want her out by May
And "Shadow" had not survived

I was there just twice before
In nineteen ninety four and five
And just as they had touched my heart
That dog and ranch had died

STRUTHIOUS FARMS
Littleton, Colorado

WHEN ONE THINKS OF "RANCHES" ONE USUALLY THINKS OF COWS AND COWBOYS, horses, old boots and beat-up pickup trucks, and the image of a "ranch dog" would most likely take on the form of an Aussie, Border collie, Catahoula hound or some sturdy cur. The term "livestock" as well, conjures up the image of herds of slow moving cattle, grazing sheep or horses scattered through fields of alfalfa. But an ostrich "flerd"? (A term jokingly used by ostrich ranchers.) Will this new breed of ranching catch on? Time will tell.

There is a growing interest in the American West, as well as in the rest of the world, in exotic ranching. For K. D. (Ken) Turnbull, making the decision to move from the city (Denver) and leave the corporate world of computer application in the oil industry behind, has turned out to be an interesting and adventurous proposition. When Ken started his ostrich operation, he had several decisions to make, one of which being what to call his business. He chose "Struthious Farms" from the scientific classification *Struthio camelus*, which means "camel bird."

According to Ken, the ostrich is potentially a great food source (though still considered an exotic delicacy). Additionally, the ostrich offers products such as leather, feathers and even ostrich oil, which is currently imported from Australia.

Also, according to the ostrich rancher, the production of this particular "livestock" (which is how it is legally classified in Colorado) is far more economical and environmentally friendly than traditional stock ranching. Needing little water, the ostrich fares well in the high desert regions of the West.

Ken also needed to educate himself in the routine care and development of these large birds, which included finding the perfect breed of dog to "guard" the stock. After reading a book on guardian breeds, he chose the Great Pyrenees, not only for its reputation as a fine guardian of its territory and stock, but also for its nickname as the "gentle giant." Ken gives tours of his farm to interested people to satisfy and educate the curious and says that many visitors end up wanting to pet and offer tidbits to the dogs. Having many groups of children attending these tours, he wanted a breed of dog that would be gentle with them. The Great Pyrenees is wary of strangers and will certainly protect against a human threat, but they seem to be able to differentiate between a non-threatening situation and one that is questionable.

Ken's first working dog was a Great Pyrenees pup which he acquired when he first began his ranching venture in 1992. Naming her Kay-Dee (after his own first initials), he and the pup learned the business together as Ken let the dog's natural guarding instincts kick in as they went. Ken says that Kay-Dee used to play with the young chicks as a pup, and they with her. A kind of imprinting occurred and Kay-Dee eventually saw the livestock as something she would protect. While the first instinct of many canines might be to chase after the birds, Kay-Dee has never done this.

The Great Pyrenees, or Pyrenean Mountain Dog, is a large breed which originated in the Pyrenees mountain range between Spain and France. They were originally bred from mastiff stock and were used to protect sheep from wolves in Europe.

Their long coat is predominantly white and quite thick. This breed, when raised in a working environment, will spend most of the day sleeping and finding shelter from the hot sun. The dog spends the nights patrolling the perimeter of its territory.

The threats from most predators to the ostrich are nocturnal. Kay-Dee's night

patrol covers fifteen acres. Among the predators in this area are mountain lions, by far the biggest threat to the larger birds. The baby and young ostriches are also prime targets for coyotes, foxes, raccoons, skunks, owls, hawks and eagles. Kay-Dee will instinctively put herself between any threat and her stock. If one of these potential marauders comes close to her boundary, Kay-Dee will sound a very specific bark as she protects her "flerd." Ken says that the ostriches have learned this particular warning sign of Kay-Dee's and the bark always sends them fleeing to a "neutral" corner of their pens, where they have learned to wait it out while the dog does her work.

Another threat to this exotic stock is the bird rustler. Ostriches are worth a lot of money, so identifying microchips are injected into them subcutaneously. If someone is caught with an ostrich and can't explain the microchip, the ostrich rustler is likely to end up in jail.

In 1995, during one of Kay-Dee's early morning patrols, a neighbor assumed the dog had wandered from home and Kay-Dee ended up at the Humane Society in Littleton, presumed to be a lost dog. When the dog failed to come back to the house that morning, Ken began his search and quickly found her impounded. While he was retrieving Kay-Dee from the shelter, he learned that they had an adult, neutered male Great Pyrenees up for adoption. He had been there for over sixty days. The dog had evidently been acquired by a city dweller who found that it was not the kind of dog to be kept in close quarters. The dog had also been debarked. His natural instinct to alert his owner of danger ended up getting the dog a trip to the surgery table, ultimately stripping him of one of his greatest gifts as a guard dog.

Ken had been thinking about getting another Great Pyrenees as a companion for Kay-Dee and to supplement the security of the stock. Ken decided to take

"Tony" back to Struthious Farms to see if he could provide a good home as Kay-Dee's working companion. Ken reports the dog was in very poor condition when he first met him, too thin and apparently very depressed. Ken's veterinarian gave the dog a clean bill of health, suggested plenty of TLC, a quality diet and time. Although it took two months before the dog began to fill out, he is now at a good body weight and slowly adjusting to his new home and job.

Ken says that Kay-Dee was at first jealous of Tony's presence, but that she has adjusted well and the two are now fast friends. The only time either dog shows any irritation with the other is at mealtime. If one finishes eating before the other and decides to saunter over to check out the other's dish, the slower eater will give a warning growl. Other than that, the two go about their patrol with enthusiasm. As dusk approaches and the temperatures cool, the two dogs begin to prance about, curled tails held high, in anticipation of their night watch. The cold Colorado winters don't seem to bother these well-insulated canines. The elements take a backseat to the obvious enjoyment these "gentle giants" exhibit while guarding their "flerd."

MY KAY

By Peggy Godfrey

Long time coming into your self-confidence
Timid among people, bold with livestock
You are the ever-moving fence behind them
Never barking, rarely nipping.
You have such good sense
Such natural affinity for your work.
When you aren't working at my command
I can trust you to sharpen your eye
But not hassle stock.
You read me well, teach me much
When you lay your head
Against my leg
I become grounded.

WINDSONG RANCH

Cayucos, California

Bsome two hundred and fifty miles north of Los Angeles, California, on the Pacific Coast Highway, is the quaint little beach town of Cayucos. It is a bit strange to travel through the trendy towns and cities on this route, with designer shops and stylish residents, and then to glance towards the ocean between the highway exits and see grazing cattle and weathered corrals barely holding up to the humid, salty air. Going east off the highway, in seconds one encounters rolling golden hills and massive sycamore trees sharing the landscape with prickly pear cactus. The fences hug the hillsides. Scattered about on the rural roads are the old ranches of the California coastline.

Kathy and Brad Warren have lived and worked on their Windsong Ranch since their marriage twenty years ago. Brad's brother and his family also live and work on the surrounding family ranch, the Flying E. Brad's family has owned land in Cayucos for generations as his grandfather moved there with his family when he was just three years old. Throughout his entire life of 102 years, he called this beautiful place home. The family leases approximately six thousand acres of land on which they run their cow/calf operations.

The Warrens have always used dogs in their ranching work and, as it happens, Kathy is a highly respected and sought-after breeder and trainer of Australian shepherds and Border collies. She breeds only working dogs and it is clear, watching the woman working with her dogs, that her breed lines have been fine-tuned to the art of herding. Kathy travels frequently with her dogs, conducting trials and

demonstrations. Third-generation Warrens on this land, daughters Melinda and Kim are also active in the trials and help out on the ranch.

The California coastline offers its share of adventurous weather patterns, and in the fall of 1997, lots of rain came to the coastal regions. On a particular day during this time, through the downpour and wind, Kathy had to bring the herd from a coastal pasture up to the corral by the barn. Brad and Kathy, in slickers, hats and mud boots, were less than thrilled to have to brave the elements, but ranch life is dictated by the weather and when stock is in trouble, the rancher must work. With help from Melinda's dog, "Salty" and another blue merle Aussie, "Eddie," Kathy mounted her horse and brought in the herd. Several mother cows had died, apparently from a problem with the feed. It was imperative to get three orphaned calves to the shelter of the barn and begin bottle feeding them. After the dogs had herded the calves out of the corral, the Warrens transported them using a four wheeler sporting a bumper sticker which reads "Cowdog Cadillac." The four wheeler is not used often, mainly to haul feed, but when it is, the dogs take advantage of the free ride. Through it all, Salty and Eddie seemed impervious to the harsh weather and seemed quite happy to be out working in the muddy fields.

Once the three calves were sheltered and being fed, the two rain-soaked dogs lay quietly on the straw-covered floor, watching Kathy's every move as she cared for the babies. The dogs seemed to know that the

excitement of their work was done for the day and settled into their down time gracefully.

The breeding kennel that Kathy operates is named, like the ranch, Windsong Kennels. She usually has about ten dogs, including pups, at any given time. While she loves Aussies and Border collies alike, she says she does have a preference for the Australian shepherd breed due to their temperament. For training purposes, she keeps a band of sheep on the ranch.

Most small ranching operations rely on outside income from other endeavors and the Windsong is no exception. Although Kathy loves her work with the kennel and Brad is employed by the State, the heart and soul of the family belongs to the ranch and their dogs. It's easy to understand the love the Warrens have for this land as one ascends the gently sloping fields to a high point on the property, where the Pacific Ocean gleams in the distance. This is the Warren's "backyard." The hustle and glitz of the populated towns of the coastline fade from memory amidst the serenity of this old ranch country. The dogs lie still as they listen to the silence and sniff the salty breeze.

RANCH DOG [as a ranch dog might tell it]

by Marianne Murdock

Now I don't go to groomers
Gettin' clipped and sprayed and fluffed
Bein' dirty's natural
A dip in the "crik's" enough
I wouldn't trade a thousand baths
For an hour in a mountain stream
The soul's what needs the cleansin'
That's the only life for me

My master doesn't carry me
Or walk me on a lead
I follow herds and horse's hooves
It's in me like a need
I wouldn't trade a thousand homes
Wherever we might be
I'm loyal to that cowpoke
That's the only life for me

And I don't eat no fancy food
From bowls bought at a store
My master gives me chow and scraps
On Mother Nature's floor
I wouldn't trade a thousand meals
For a scrap that is my fee
Gatherin' 'round a campfire
That's the only life for me

And I don't chase no tennis balls
Or squeaky kinds of toys
Two thousand pounds of beef I'll chase
With cowgirls and cowboys
I wouldn't trade a thousand bones
For one day herdin' free
Chasin' after cattle
That's the only life for me

And when the stars come out at night
At the end of a workin' day
No fancy basket for my sleep
Just a patch of grass or hay
I wouldn't trade a thousand beds
For sleep beneath a tree
To smell the open sweet night air
That's the only life for me

And I won't have no sterile cage
When old age creeps on up
I'll retire at the homestead
Where I started as a pup
I wouldn't trade a thousand cures
For nature's remedy
I'll live and die a ranch dog
That's the only life for me

P BAR RANCH

Kirkland, Arizona

P A BEAUTIFUL HIGH DESERT VALLEY SPREADS ALONG THE WINDING BOUNDARIES OF THE Hassayampa River in west central Arizona. This is Arizona ranch country. Among the ten ranches owned by the Maughn family are the P Bar and Cross S spreads. These two ranches comprise approximately sixty-four thousand acres of private and leased land. Situated nearby in the surprisingly green area of Walnut Grove is the ranch manager's home. Neil and Mary Abbott run a mixed Brangus and Hereford cattle operation. The Abbotts have been ranching together since 1980. Anyone spending time with this couple would quickly agree they've chosen the lifestyle that suits them best .

Neil Abbott was born and raised in north-ern Michigan to a rancher father and a ranch cook mother. He says he bought his first cow at the age of thirteen, even before buying his first horse. Ranching has taken him to many areas throughout the West. Neil was working as a farrier when he met Mary. She was train-ing and showing horses at the time and was one of his customers. Neil says that "Mary knew a good thing when she looked at it, and

now I shoe her horses for nothing." She had never run cattle before but once she and Neil fell in love, she became a quick study. When it comes to "cowboyin'," Neil says that "good or bad, whatever she learned, she learned most of it from me." If that's the case, to watch this woman work, one would have to surmise that Neil is a pretty good teacher.

On the P Bar Ranch, the cattle usually winter in the Kirkland Valley where the climate is milder than on the other side of the mountains. This is where Neil and Mary have their home base, not only for themselves but for their family of working dogs (currently numbering eight), a mule and seven horses. The ranch house is quiet and unassuming. On the kitchen table sits an old mason jar with one single, perfect red rose. Neil apparently noticed the bloom that morning on his way back up to the house after checking on the cattle. He says when he saw it, he knew Mary had to have it. In the kitchen on the refrigerator is tacked a note that reads: "It is what we value, not what we have, that makes us rich." It is clear that life slows down a bit as the winter months approach and the cattle have been moved to winter pasture.

The hot Arizona summer months find the Abbotts and their herd up in the mountains and cool pines in an area called Wolf Creek. The high desert heat is tempered by the tall evergreens and the altitude. They drive the cattle from winter pasture to the designated areas, usually with the help of one other cowhand, and set up a base camp from which to work through the summer. They typically use all seven horses, the mule and their eight dogs to do the work. They rotate the animals so that none is overworked. "The only thing that don't get rotated are the saddles and the riders," they tell us.

As the Abbotts sit drinking coffee on a crisp fall morning at the base camp in

Wolf Creek, there are several different breeds of cowdog tethered around the camp. The younger dogs have not yet learned not to run off after things. "Shorty," a fourteen-year-old Queensland heeler who is now retired, is the Abbott's favorite dog. They say he has probably traveled "a million miles behind a horse." Neil says the old dog is "deaf as a post" now, but it doesn't seem to handicap him in any way. Having free run of the base camp, Shorty is most content to follow Neil or Mary around as they go about their chores, or to simply lie beside the campfire and nap.

The other adult dogs at base camp want nothing more than to work, work, work. The anticipation shows in their eyes. They have all been trained to their various areas of expertise.

Three of the dogs, "Rip" a five-year-old heeler, "Ken," a four-year-old Aussie and "Buck," a one-year-old Aussie mix, are all "drivers," which means that they keep the cattle moving. There are four "catch" dogs, all Catahoulas, named "Alija," a fifteen-month-old, "Bub," a thirteen-month-old, "Gator," a three-year-old and "Whetto," a thirteen-month-old pure white male with blue eyes. The catch dogs are all pretty eager and Neil says that Gator will "use himself up like a sixteen-year-old boy." This is one reason for the rotations. Mary is getting ready to go out over the mountain to find some stray cattle. She will take two catch dogs with her today and use the other two tomorrow. This gives the animals a much needed rest in this kind of work, where many miles are covered over rough country. Ken is one of the best dogs of the lot, and although he is trained as a driver, Mary says she uses him frequently when looking for strays because he is excellent at alerting her to the presence of loners that have separated from the herd.

The Abbotts usually train a new pup with two experienced dogs and find that the young canines are eager to join in the activities and mimic the behavior of the older dogs. The country in which they work is perilous. Neil and Mary both feel that the Catahoula is well suited for this kind of work because of its strength and ruggedness. During the physically taxing seasons, the two also switch the working dogs to a higher protein feed to give them that extra "get up an' go."

Mary has her horse saddled up and her supplies and dogs ready to go. As she climbs into the saddle, Alija and Ken are stationed, one on either side of the mare, waiting for the sign of departure. The other dogs are obviously anxious to join them, but that would defeat the purpose. The cowgirl will ride into Slate Creek with the dogs in hopes of bringing back the stray cattle. If all goes well, they will return to base camp by five or six in the evening. The dogs will be glad to get back to camp and will tell the others, the way dogs do, about their adventure. Mary will sit by the fire with a hot cup of coffee, pull her boots off and replace them with Birkenstocks, and after the horses, dogs (and people) have been fed, she and Neil will enjoy the night sounds and smells of the peaceful pine forest.

CHASING RABBITS

by Marianne Murdock

Night falls
Black/white
coats glistening

Sleeping
still listening

Through the chilled
night air

Hard day
herding

Nothing moves

Full bellies
heavy
in the snow

Nothing moves

But the
muddy feet
heavy eyes

of dogs dreaming

ZEILER RANCH
Wheatland, Wyoming

The "wanna-be's." They're dogs, and they live on a ranch, a true ranch. They know how to chase things. They're loyal to their master. There are cattle and horses on the property around which they appear to be fearless. So what's the problem? Well, perhaps for five of these dogs, it's simply a matter of bloodline. Sure, there are two, "Jethro" and "Fox," who obviously have cowdog-laced genes, but what about "Casey" the Samoyed, "Zach" and "Zima" the Husky/malamute litter mates, "Ben" the West Highland terrier and "Chester" the Chihuahua/terrier mix? Then again, maybe it's got something to do with the ranch owners, Dave and Donna Zeiler. Dr. Zeiler is a veterinarian who escaped the demands of a private practice on the outskirts of Washington, D.C. about nine years ago. Deciding to return to his roots in the West and a simpler lifestyle, he and his wife packed up their belongings and various pets in search of a ranch in the Colorado/Wyoming area. They settled on a pristine parcel of 3,400 acres, 35 miles southwest of the small town of Wheatland, Wyoming.

Starting out as cattle ranchers with a herd of Beef Blacks and Black Baldie cattle, the two set about their new life as true westerners. However, Dave's veterinary expertise soon beckoned him to the trials and tribulations of the area's wildlife population. He quickly found himself busy as a research veterinarian at the Sybille unit of the Wyoming Game and Fish Department. The cattle business soon took second billing and the two animal lovers, before they knew what hit them, had accumulated an array of family pets which usually found their way to the Zeiler Ranch because of some medical or behavioral malady which the previous owners were sure the vet could handle. The menagerie presently includes "Gary" and "Gordon," two gigantic draft horses, "Bugs" and "Canadian," two Arabian horses who traveled west with the Zeilers, "Sal" the quarter horse, the latest addition "Lily," a small, eighteen-year-old bay mare, "Pepsi" and "James," the two goats, eighteen cats, four ferrets and, of course, the dogs.

Contrary to the image the Lazy S brand brings to mind, there is little time for laziness when caring for this many animals on a daily basis. If nothing else, the pack of canines offers loyal companionship to Dave and Donna as they go about their business of "running the ranch" and enjoying the secluded serenity of this land.

The grazing land is presently leased out to another cattle rancher, but Dave and Donna are now making plans to begin ranching again. Although they haven't yet decided on their "livestock of choice," they are considering buffalo as well as cattle. And what about Jethro, Fox, Casey, Zach, Zima, Ben and Chester? Will they be an integral part of the work force once this happens? Well, Donna says they're getting pretty adept at keeping the cats in check and they occasionally take a curious (if cautious) interest in supervising the existence of the two 2,000 pound draft horses. She also reports that Jethro has recently taken on the role of guardian, alerting the clan to would-be coyote intruders, and Zach has twice warned them of the presence of snakes near the homestead.

But will they become true Ranch Dogs? Will they ever know the correct response to directions such as "herd 'em," "catch 'em" or "hold 'em up"? Well, maybe, with a little time and some training, but just maybe. For the moment, the Zeilers, who don't seem to be able to say no to a canine in need, are content to simply share their ranch with these very happy animals.

ST. LAZARUS OF THE DOGS[†]

by Sharlot Hall

When I am Come to Heaven's door
   (God grant that door to me!)
Right well I know the Saint that first
   My eyes will long to see.
To Peter, Keeper of that Door,
   I'll bend my head in thanks,
And I shall know Great Michael, high
   Above the angel ranks.

But I shall seek a grassy bank
   Beneath a leafy tree
And there I'll find Saint Lazarus,
   A great hound at his knee...
A tawny hound, all russet gold
   With eyes so brown and deep
That all the love we shared on earth
   His look will surely keep.

And well I know Saint Lazarus
   Will lift a gentle hand
And bid me sit beside him there
   Upon the shining sand.
And that great tawny head will press
   Down hard upon my arm,
That golden flank sway close to me
   To keep me from alarm.

†Reprinted with permission from the
Sharlot Hall Museum

CHUCK SHEPPARD

Prescott, Arizona

CHUCK SHEPPARD WAS BORN IN GLOBE, ARIZONA. A RODEOER AT THE AGE OF sixteen, he found himself training horses twenty-four years later. He eventually drifted into ranching, and, for years, ran the Kieckhefer Ranch in Prescott, Arizona.

At the age of eighty-two, Chuck leases a small piece of land out by Willow Lake in Prescott. With the help of his one and only cow dog, a black mouth cur by the name of "Blondie," this traditional cowboy runs about fifty head of cattle.

The black mouth cur is a sturdy, short-coated dog with course hair. Coloring ranges from reddish gold to fawn or yellow, usually with a black muzzle or mask. This dog is known in the southeastern United States for it's excellent hunting skills, but it also makes a fine herding dog.

Blondie is about nine years old and Chuck likes to move cattle with her and his horse "Baby Doll." He's a one dog man when he's working and that's the way he likes it. He says this dog will "stop 'em, hold 'em up and won't bite 'em!" (Like some Catahoulas he's known!) When Blondie finds a stray, she'll bay and circle, letting her master know she's done her job well.

According to Chuck, if a calf gets separated from its mother, it will go back to the last place that it suckled. If given the chance, the mother will also return to find her calf. Blondie has a way of sniffing out these lost babies.

Through a combination of whistles and grunts, Chuck can communicate exactly what he wants from his dog. It's obvious, watching the two work together, that this dog is loyal to only one man, barely letting strangers get within twenty feet of her. The minute Chuck lets out a whistle, Blondie is away and in the horse trailer with Baby Doll, anxiously waiting for the ride out to the range land to do what she does best.

This cowboy, who claims to be "half Morman, half Texan," has a lifelong workmate for the business of running cattle, not to mention a loyal friend. Chuck says, "'bout the only time this dog would leave me or the barn, is when the wife would yell out the back door with a pan full of table scraps." They live a simple life, and that suits Chuck and Blondie just fine.

A Miracle

By Peggy Godfrey

Last Spring I began riding two herds of cows who were calving. An icy, muddy, windy seven weeks kept me horseback and checking regular for difficult births, abandoned and sick babies. Both my dogs went with me, staying back when I needed to ride close to cows with new calves. By the time the weather warmed, both herds were accustomed to seeing the dogs.

Later, when moving cattle from pasture to pasture, the dogs helped me herd. Kay, a Border collie, works the cattle gently and with finesse. Her attentive responses to my commands are instant. Dingo stays by my horse until directed to help. Her style is on the order of a guided missile. After a couple of successful maneuvers, Dingo grew deaf to my commands. Her zeal to move the herd with nipping and barking took precedence over obedience.

One morning I hollered and threatened to make sausage out of her too many times to suit me. Next day I left her home. She moaned, sulked and pouted. On the third day, I let her go with me again. What a miracle! Her deafness was completely healed. Obedient, attentive — she developed into dependable help.

Herding is an inborn trait in many breeds of dogs. Town and city living, as well as a non-working rural life, can be extremely frustrating for these animals. This accounts for a great deal of the mischief they cause.

Whether man or beast, finding the best work to express innate abilities and energy results in effective living, and resonates with freedom.

MAGGIE CREEK RANCH
Elko, Nevada

THE MAGGIE CREEK RANCH IS ONE OF THE LARGEST CATTLE OPERATIONS IN THE WEST. Running forty miles north to south and twenty miles wide along Maggie Creek outside of Elko, Nevada, it is also peppered with many smaller ranches that make up this expansive spread. The ranch produces Semitole/Gelbie and Hereford/Angus breeds of cattle. The manager of Maggie Creek, Wayne Fahsoltz, has been running this operation since 1986 and says he's used working dogs all his life. He and his wife, Judi, raise Border collies and have been breeding his dog "Sam" with Judi's dog "Katie" with impressive results. Sam has sired more than a few of the working dogs on the Maggie Creek and these particular cowdog pups are sought after by other ranchers throughout the West.

The Border collie, which originates from Great Britain, is not quite the stocky, physically imposing mass as are many of the other breeds of cowdogs. However, the graceful and magnificent moves of this breed, which seem to be genetically choreographed, are second to none and demand the respect of even the most formidable livestock.

Wayne employs an unusual method of training the young pups. Using small flocks of Indian running ducks, he slowly coaxes the natural herding instincts out of these young dogs as they learn to "herd" the ducks, preparing them for the real work of moving cattle. It's a gentler way to train and cuts down on "accidents." By the time the dogs are ready to confront

their first bovine charge, they have already learned their commands and have been kept well in check by their trainer.

There are many hands on the Maggie Creek and they all use dogs in their work. One of the young ranch hands working around the headquarters is Jon. He works with his two Border collies, "Mattie" and "Mo," who are impressive herders and very attached to their owner. While many cowboys use voice commands to instruct their dogs, Jon has trained his two to respond to his whistles.

One of the smaller ranches on the Maggie Creek is Red House Ranch, situated in the rolling hills and low-lying brush north of ranch headquarters. The charming old house on the property serves as the home for Royce and Laurel Hansen. Royce has been working cattle ranches for most of his life and has been at the Red House Ranch since 1988. While much of his job now is caretaking the property, he still sees to the cattle when needed. Most of the herd is shipped out to milder climates during the harsh Nevada winters, but Royce will occasionally care for as many as 700 head at the Red House. He also serves as cook for the crew during branding season. Royce's culinary specialty (according to the man himself) is "beans & meat," but he says he can whip up a mean egg sandwich in a pinch.

One can find ranch dogs all around the Red House Ranch. Royce's dogs are not purebred, and he does have quite a variety. One of his favorites is a six-year-old

kelpie/Border collie mix named Jenny. It's pretty clear when you see the two together that Jenny's sweet on Royce as well. He says she's getting a little stiff now so he doesn't use her as much as he used to. Her loyalty is obvious, though, and she is content to simply be there, working or not.

Royce says one of his favorite breeds over the years has been the kelpie. Originally from Austria, this dog is known for its energy, stamina and the ability to work in arid regions where the next watering hole could be miles away.

Another breed that Royce would like to try out is the Catahoula. Seems he's heard of their strength and what he calls their "kamikaze" approach to herding cattle. Royce likes to get a dog and take it out to the Red House Ranch just to see what it's made of. He's not accustomed to formal training and prefers to use his intuition and experience when it comes to choosing dogs for work. Of course, another situation also occurs that might produce a ranch dog. Royce had a ranching friend visiting a while back who brought his Border collie/Aussie male with him. Royce says the fellow was meaning to have the dog neutered but before he got around to it, the dog fathered a litter of pups with one of the Red House dogs. Being an unplanned event, Royce refers to the whole incident as a "teenage deal." The pups are spending their first few months in the abandoned chicken coop with their mother and Royce has already picked out names for two of them. "Shorty" for the pup born with a stubbed tail and "Chipper" for a pup with just the opposite; his long tail never stops wagging! Laurel is a true animal lover, so naturally, many of these surprise additions end up "homesteading" with the Hansens. It's also obvious that the cowboy enjoys the pups.

It all sounds like a pretty good "gig" when Royce says that some days he'll walk out of the house in his slippers and send two or three dogs out to bring the cattle up to him. The bottom line, according to this man, is that "no cow is gonna stop for him, but they'll sure as hell stop for a couple of dogs."

THUNDER AND LIGHTNIN'

By Dee Strickland Johnson

"How come you keep that worthless hound?"
　　Sez a new ranch hand one day.
"That lazy one, ol' Lightnin'
　　Potlicker don't earn his pay!
He'd ought to be good for somethin';
　　Looks border collie from the back,
But all he does is tag them kids —
　　Why he's a lap dog there to Jack!"

"Well" says I, "I'll tell you a story
　　'Bout two little mongrel pups,
We called 'em Thunder and Lightnin' —
　　Seemed pretty good names to us.

Now Thunder trained up easy;
　　Learned quick to handle stock.
She retrieves them when they wander
　　And she heels them when they balk.
And Thunder could frighten a ragin' bull
　　With that loud persistent bark,
While Lightnin' was no 'count on the range—
　　Right from the very start,

"Yep, Thunder lived up to her name,
　　But Lightnin's a joke for him
(Like you call a big man Tiny
　　Or a really fat guy slim).

"Jackie was barely walkin —
　　Just toddlin' on the ground —
When one day Ann heard a rattle:
　　That high spine-chillin' sound,
And then she heard lil' Jackie scream,
　　And Thunder set up a roar,
And Lightnin' was off with the speed of light,
　　Like he'd never run before.

"He knocked Jack on his little fat rump
　　And he run 'twixt him and that snake
And he grabbed that reptile by the throat
　　And he begun to shake
that thing! (I reckon a snake might be all throat,
　　Now that it comes to mind,
But I'd best get back to my story
　　'fore it gets left behind)."

"No, I don't mind feedin' that lazy mutt
　　As he sprawls 'neath his tamarack.
If it wasn't for ol' Lightnin',
　　We wouldn't have our Jack."

"Why, before I'd give up Lightnin'
　　I'd lose my horse and everything!
Now, Thunder is a good cow dog,
　　But Lightnin'— he's the king!"

For Bill and Pokie

The Spirits Of Dogs

by Marianne Murdock

Out here in the vast landscapes
The big sky
The cool, eager streams
Running, leaping, playing, resting
Are the spirits of dogs

Dogs who've been there, done that
Dogs who, along with their masters
Have dreamed of freedom
of Nature's kaleidoscope of beauty
Smells, textures, sights
Warmth, movement, music
Pulled at us,
Me and my dogs
My man

We didn't make it to the ranch, boys
But we visited
Trouble is, once you taste it
You always want more
Need more
I still dream of the open spaces

My dogs have since passed on
Become the Earth
Sorry boys
Time slips right by

I still think of you doing what you did best
Being ALIVE, Being LOVE
Taking the seasons as they came
And shaking off the tread

Unquestionable love
Whatever that is
You had it
For everything good
For your people
Death, the only thing strong enough
to lure you away
Unlike the man

Somewhere
Out here in the West
The spirits of dogs dance in my heart